Long Ago in Oregon

Long Ago in Oregon

by Claudia Lewis

pictures by Joel Fontaine

A TRUMPET CLUB SPECIAL EDITION

Published by
The Trumpet Club
1 Dag Hammarskjold Plaza
New York, New York 10017

Dell ® TM 681510, Dell Publishing Co., Inc.

All ages

ISBN: 0-440-84174-7

Reprinted by arrangement with Harper & Row, Publishers Inc.

Printed in the United States of America

October 1987

10 9 8 7 6 5 4 3 2 1

CW

*To the memory of my parents
and to my three brothers and sister
with love*

April 19, 1918

Contents

Our Family,
One Summer Day
1917

There! I put the pencil down—
Another chapter done
in "Little Ella"
for my brother's magazine.
I draw the pictures and write stories,
he writes jokes and riddles
and types it all,
and binds it into shape with string.
Best Stories is the name.

I hear my brothers outdoors
playing Little Army,
chasing around and drilling.
I think the oldest one would really like
to be a soldier in the war
against the Germans overseas,
marching and shouting out commands (not killing).

And I hear Mamma now upstairs
with my little sister
waking from her nap.
So, what shall I do
for an hour, this sunny afternoon?
Stop for Madge across the street and
skate!
all around the town—
We know the sidewalks best for skates,
the smoothest ones.

Later on,
when Papa comes from his office
up on College Hill,
perhaps he'll bring a watermelon home
big enough for us all—
our family and any neighbor children
playing here still.

I know that after supper
we're all going to ride
out of town, to the little hill
where we stop the car
and look out over that wide valley
filled with fields
below the distant mountains
up and down the coast.
(The ocean's over there—
the beach!)

And we'll stay a while
to watch the setting sun
light up the sky and hills
and planted fields—

Then home to bed, alas,
before it's really night.
The new-cut grass around the house
smells sweet—
and from our sleeping porch
we hear with longing
calls of Run, Sheep, Run
and Hide-and-Seek—
shouts of other children playing
in the dimming light.

But Mamma comes
with kisses and good-night,
and soon we fall asleep,
as over us the cup of sky
resounds more faintly with calls
and cries far away...far away...

The Woodsaw

Suddenly
in the early morning
SCRE-E-E-CH!
The woodsaw
scratching the sky!

Rush out—
Follow—
Find it—

There!
By Lane's woodpile.

Two men
lift the log,
shove to whirring wheel—
        SCRE-E-E-CH!
        Zup!

Move it over
        SCRE-E-E-CH!
        Zup!

Hoist another
SCRE-E-E-CH!
Zup!

The sawmill noise
has brought
all the neighborhood
girls and boys out
to watch the giant cutter
slice through wood
as easily
as a knife cuts cake
or soft brown bread
or butter.

We could stay
all day
staring!

Coincidence

My mother's best friend
from around the block
would pop in the door
without ringing
or knocking
but always called out
"Hoo Hoo!"

One day, bringing a pie,
she called
"Hoo Hoo!"
just as the bird in our clock
sprang out and sang
"Cuckoo!"

We never forgot!

The Farmers
and the Snakes

When the Johnsons took me
with them
for a weekend at their farm
near Old Baldy mountain,
the buggy ride out of town
was fun.

But there,
around the summer house,
snakes were sliding in the weedy grass,
long, thick snakes.

Men from the farm
came with scythes
to slash the weeds
and hook up snakes and toss them
into a roaring fire,
to make the grass safe for us.

10

I could not have told
which froze me most,
the crawling snakes
or sight of them flung
to bonfire death.

The Nelsons

I

In the early mornings
Mr. Nelson passed our house
on his walk,
in his neat dark suit
and coat, open and
flying a bit;
white hair,
sideburns,
stepping along
swinging umbrella
for a cane.
When Mr. Nelson walked
he *walked*,
enjoying the air
and the morning.

Everyone knew
his big store
was the best in town.
Always at Christmas
a Santa there
had gifts for children.

When I was very small
we lived close by. —
Mrs. Nelson, plump and cozy
like a grandma,
would invite us in on days
when she made marshmallows.
Marshmallows! Not like
the puffs we bought in boxes
but trembling, glistening white,
arranged in fragile pieces
on a tray.

And her grown-up boys
and girls would play with us,
swing and toss us
in the yard
all around the snowball tree.

Far in the back of my mind
as time passed
I remembered once in a while—
almost not at all—
that the Nelsons were Catholics.

Mother had told us
any church in town
was all right for us—
except the Catholic.
"Why not the Catholic?"
"...Well, in that church
they worship images."

What did this have to do
with the snowball tree,
with cozy marshmallow grandma,
and the jaunty man—
the gentleman—
who walked in the morning?

I never even tried
to fit these pieces together.

II
One day I realized
I hadn't seen him lately,
passing by.
"Mother, where is Mr. Nelson?"

"Oh, I meant to tell you.
We won't see him anymore—
He was old, very old,
...He has died..."

(Meant to tell me?
I don't think you did.)

Died—
    I glimpse a great darkness
    in spite of angels.

Dying?
    I've heard snatches
    of sad talk.
    Now I know—

Death
    is Mr. Nelson
    striding along
    alone
    in the morning
    toward something black and far
    in the night.

Growing Up

It was clear to see
that in our town
there were girls
who wore short dresses
and ladies who wore long.
No people in between.
Our hired girls weren't girls;
they were women, grown.
And so were the ladies
up at the college—
students, yes, but tall,
and soft as mothers,
hair piled high,
skirts long.

One afternoon
I thought of me
no longer small,
a lady, too, some day.
How? When?

"Mother!" I ran to ask.
"Will it happen
suddenly
that I shoot up tall?
Will I stand waiting
in your bedroom,
holding my ripped
little dress around me,
my underwear all in shreds,
while you rush
to Nelson's
to buy me a corset
and all I need
to be a lady?"
"No, no, no," she laughed,
and told me
how I would grow up
year by year
slowly,
as I had always grown.

So she said.
But still I wondered
about that first long skirt
and the corset.
When?

Christmas Trees

We were never in the Blairs' house
across the street
except at Christmas.
The two daughters there
were ladies
in long dresses,
much too old to play with us.
But at Christmas
"Come in," they always said,
"Come in and see our tree."

We stood there in the living room
staring—
The great tree, touching the ceiling,
was no longer a tree—
It was a shape
covered with ornaments—
pictures, trinkets, embroidered balls,
saints and angels, plastered on
all over—
and no branches visible at all.

I stood smiling,
polite,
never speaking my thought:

> Why do they trim a tree
> this way?
> Our tree is trimmed
> the way a tree should be,
> with tinsel draping across
> and popcorn chains;
> little glass fruits and lanterns
> red and gold,
> dangling,
> and candles on the branches.

Yes, a wonderful tree!

At the Graveyard
on Decoration Day

On Decoration Day
children in our school
marched
in the town parade
to decorate the graves
of old soldiers.
Down Madison to Third
in the middle of the street
we walked,
waving little flags
and stepping to the beat
of big drums.

When we crossed the bridge
we were there
and had to listen for a while
to speeches.

But then
my friend Jeannette and I
prowled around the old graveyard
overrun with grasses.
Let the grown-ups
talk of soldiers
and the Civil War—
What we hunted for,
under tangled briars,
were graves of little children
(why did they die so young?)
little children we had never known.

No Dimes

In our family
no rewards
for good report cards.
"We expect you
to do well—
No reason to reward you,"
our parents said.

We knew they took pride
in us, no matter what;
we understood about the grades;
agreed—
And yet—all the other kids...

When those good reports
came around
we ran next door
to show Mrs. Tate.
She had no children of her own,
she loved us,
and we always came away
from her kitchen
with an orange
or a cookie,
when she had seen
all those 95's and 98's.

Cookies weren't dimes,
cookies weren't rewards,
weren't they O.K.?

Outdoors

I

Oh tumbling joy
of the mustard field,
the vacant lot
next to Jackson's—
Rip through, run,
lie down and roll
in the sweet
bitter taste of yellow—
Gobble blossoms!

My favorite place—
the hidden den
in the shrubbery,
where I creep in
and sit with my
book
and my doll
Gwendolyn,
　　and my little
　　striped bag
　　of jelly beans
　　from Horning's.

The New Girl

At Central School
we played in the basement
when it rained.
There on the girls' side
ladders were hung
from the ceiling
to swing on.

One day the new girl
was swinging there—
I could see she had on
a union suit
and no bloomers—
"I hate my mother!"
she suddenly shouted out.

"How could you
hate your *mother*?"

"I do—
I hate her!"

Upside-down world!
As though two and two
no longer made four;
as though eggs did not break
into yellows and whites—

I went home
and told my precious mother.

Not in a Hundred Years

In fourth grade
one boy,
Milton,
couldn't read.

Gawky,
tall, and thin,
when it was his turn
he would stand,
fumble with a word or two,
then sit down again.

Hopeless!

But one day
a few words came,
then a few more.
Our teacher stood,
moved near.
"Yes, yes, that's right!
You can read it,
Milton!"

He went on,
stumbling,
but words came.
"Of course! Of course!
Keep going, Milton!
I knew you could—
And now the next word,
starts with 'm' just like your name—

"Yes— Yes—
Go on!
Good!"

Every one of us
sat listening,
watching,
as Miss Baldwin
pushed words
out of Milton,
prompting,
urging.

She waved her arms,
her voice rose
and rose.
And I suddenly sat
glued to my desk,
amazed, seeing what I never dreamed
to see, in a hundred years,
great tears
in my teacher's eyes.

The Blue Bird

(BY MAETERLINCK)

The day had come!
We were ready to leave
with my father
to hear Mother's "Reading,"
The Blue Bird,
story I loved,
mysterious.

I in my best pink dress
and the two little boys
in white,
but not the oldest brother—
He wouldn't come,
he stayed at home
and never told us why.

40

(But didn't I know?
I, too, was scared
and filled with dread—
I, too, almost didn't want to go.
Mother might forget!
Mother might forget!
There she'd be,
up on the stage,
everyone staring
while she was stumbling,
standing alone,
our lovely mother
in her long, green gown.
And how could she know
by heart
all the words of this book?
True, she had been practicing—
I'd heard her mumbling
around the house
as she ironed
and worked.)

At the church we sat
up high,
first row,
looking right down
on the stage
where she would come
and bow, and stand
by the flowers.
I sat small,
hiding myself a bit.
(Mother, don't forget!)

Oh, here she comes
in the long green gown,
smiling,
bowing,
    and begins.

......Why,
she's happy standing there,
anyone could tell—
......

She sounds like Mother,
speaking—
......

She knows the words!
......

Why, of course, she knows them
all very well—
......

She won't forget.
Why did I worry?
Now I am certain.
Now I can sit
and listen
to the mysterious story.

Driving Home
from Rock Creek
in the Buick

Packed close
in the back seat—
wild lilies in our hands, drooping—
myself and brothers,
baby in front
with Mother and Father.
Nearly home—
We've reached the town.

Happy with our summer day
of wading, and our homemade
blackberry ice cream—

(Down on our ankles
still the water slapping,
feet still gripping
rocks on the bottom of the stream.
Forest dark and cool around us—)

Oh—here we are,
lovely day gone—

    (Dull to be home
    while mountain air
    still clings, and sparkling
    water splashes.)

Car slowing down
to turn in—

NO! NO!
Papa's trick again—
We're going on!
(He likes to fool us—
Never tells us when.)

We screech and shout
and bump around with joy—
Riding on!
Where? Who can say?
A block or two,
not far—
But here we go,
driving right past
our own home,
stretching
the happy day,
adding time—

Who cares now
that night will come?

"Over There"

There came a time when
we knew there was a war
overseas, and young men
from our town—"boys"—
were going over.

We despised the cruel Huns,
and all through the neighborhood
sang a silly song
about canning the Kaiser.

In the sixth grade
we knitted squares
for blankets for the soldiers,
and the school asked me
to play the piano in the hall
in the morning,
when everyone marched in.
I pounded out "Joan of Arc"—
(Loved the wartime words
and tune.)

Then one day
when we were all at home
for lunch,
our father told us,
"We want you to know.
I've had to sign up
for the draft. It doesn't mean
I'm going over right now,
but someday I may have to go."
Our father, face to face
with the Huns?
Our father, shooting
and killing, and maybe
shot down?

We were deathly still.
Terror had moved near
and hunched there,
pushing
on our door.

Armistice Day, World War I

November 11, 1918

In the early morning
we heard the ringing bells
and whistles—signals
to everyone in town:
The end had come!
The armistice was signed!

We children dashed
out to our alley
with dishpans and spoons,
and banged and banged,
running up and down—
It's over!
The soldiers will be home—
We've won—
They've signed!

Later in the day, parades
and rides around.
For now, the kids
are out with sticks
and drums—Bang!
to celebrate—
It's over!
No more war!
They've signed!

Moving to Salem

I grabbed up my little sister,
not quite three.
She mustn't forget!
Around the house we went,
to remember.

"Here's the fireplace
where we hung our stockings
the night before Christmas—
Don't forget!
The bench on this side
for our toys,
and on the other side—
the wood's in there.

"And then the den—
Mamma's fern by the windows,
Papa's desk,
and behind it all our books—
Will you remember?
Here on the wall our telephone,
and now the dining room—"

So we went,
upstairs and down,
our good-bye
to this house
forever.

Glad to move
to the big new home—
Our parents said we'd love
the lawn around
and the great black walnut tree
where we'd have a swing.
And we'd love the city, too, they said,
Salem, full of roses
and forests in the parks,
and orchards on the hills
near town.

Yet, our house here is home
and we are leaving—
Don't forget!
This is forever—
We won't be back.

Claudia Lewis began writing poems at the age of ten and says that she is still learning about poetry to this day. She was connected with Bank Street College and the New School for many years as a teacher in the fields of children's literature and children of other cultures.

Joel Fontaine is a theatrical set designer as well as an illustrator. He was born in San Francisco, California, and he now lives with his wife in Brooklyn, New York.